Where the Rocks Float

MARY O'MALLEY

Where the Rocks Float

SALMON  POETRY

First published in 1993 by
Salmon Publishing Ltd.
A division of Poolbeg Enterprises Ltd,
123 Baldoyle Industrial Estate, Dublin 13, Ireland.

A catalogue record for this book is available from the British Library.

ISBN 1 897648 02 2

Cover artwork: detail from a painting by Axel Miret
Back Cover photograph by Joe O'Shaughnessy
Cover design by Poolbeg Group Services Ltd.
Set by Mac Book Limited in Palatino
Printing by the Guernsey Press Limited,
Vale, Guernsey, Channel Islands.

To the memory of Máire Bean Uí Mháille,
my grandmother

Acknowledgements are due to the following publications in which
a number of these poems first appeared:
*Krino, The Salmon Magazine, Hidden Connemara, and to RTE Radio,
RTE Television, and BBC Radio 4 where many of them were broadcast.*

I wish to thank the Arts Council for a grant to finish this
work and the Tyrone Guthrie Centre at Annaghmakerrig
where I began it.

SALMON PUBLISHING LIMITED

receives financial assistance from the

Arts Council/An Chomhairle Ealaíon.

·

Contents

III — The Boat Poems

IV — The Grannuaile Poems

I - *Ave*

" Yo no sabía qué decir, mi boca
no sabía
nombrar,
mis ojos eran ciegos,
y algo golpeaba en mi alma,
fiebre o alas perdidas,
y me fui haciendo solo,
descifrando
acquella quemadura,
y escribí la primera línea vaga, ..."

Pablo Neruda
'La Poesía'

TRIBUTE

We caravanned in the rain to Omagh. The children
were let drive, mad, across the strand.
The piper stayed behind but the thread
of his wild playing held us still.
We made an odd crowd at Feichín's well
and later clumped around a raw excavation.

As we stood there trespassing on the dead
divided between bodies and bones,
the climbers always at the edge,
I, breath-heavy, could not lay my hand
on a single wild flower, only a wreath of shells.

i

THE VISIT

The little girl tightened
the belt on her skimpy
homemade cotton dress,
knowing her clothes marked her,
that even her polished shoes were wrong.
But she smiled as she burned,
shame corseted her frame,
buckled the words
coming out of her mouth,
making even her accent a misshapen thing.

She longed and she hated
but she spoke
every time one of them came
graciously, to visit her mother.

ii

THE FOREIGNER

He had the voice of an Englishman,
wherever he got the name.
He was English to the look in his eyes.
He talked with the voice of sureness,
the voice of governors,
the voice of arrogance,
the seductive cadence of power.

He knew words of ballads
but he spoke them in the voice
of high opera.

An accent like that
is a dangerous thing,
lethal as opium.
You could get addicted
to a voice like that,
an accent
to intimidate the sea itself.

PEASANTS

Her uncle said they were all
a shower of English feckers
that should be shot. Useless
to the earth and all that walked it.
That shower
thought we were still peasants.

Isn't a peasant a bird,
a lovely shiny bird
that lives in trees
and gets shot? Not far off
her uncle said.

AVE

The little girl played
in her overturned boat,
her church, her shop, her sailing ship.
The only architecture she knew
had the vaulted roof
of a sawn in two pucán.
She plainchanted with the cuckoo
and *Ave, Ave, Ave Maria*
was the song she learned at school.

When they asked how many children
she could see the pained looks
overcome the breeding.
She felt like scabies or the mange,
Infectious and poor.

THE WORDSMITH

He was a great poet,
she a woman of little substance
when they met. She found him generous,
a courteous man with a wicked mouth.

She thought she had done
with old wounds, that history
could become that
when he gave her a book.

She didn't know
what wild horses would rear
from its innocent pages—
the fabulous beasts of the past.

vi

STRANDED

The gift had a blood price.
It landed me back
among fishermen and Englishmen,
drove me out to Trá Mhór.
I never thought to find myself like this,
thrown up like flotsam at thirty-three,
searching for God among the windfall
on a wild evening shore.

THE ROCKS

So there you are
the interloping Englishman,
you that put smacht on the sea
mapped out the roads
necessary to your kingdom.
I used to think you
a wild black-haired man.

Even here with such a shifting
you built your poems
on the foundation stones
of an empire. No wonder
they could bolt and buckle
without breaking up on the rocks.

I have only passion and despair,
nebulous things to work with,
not manly tools.

LONGING

They came in lovely leathery cars
from their big houses
being nice. What was the evening line
of roofless coastguard stations
black against the bedtime sky
to them, or the round towers
of Slyne Head?

They had pillars and porticoes
and Georgian houses where they sat
speaking of Beethoven and Bach.
They listened to golden music
at nightfall, and they knew
what each instrument was called.

The little girl twisted.
When they were gone she asked God
for the gift of tongues.

THE SHAPE OF SAYING

They call it Received English
as if it was a gift you got
by dint of primogeniture.
Maybe it was. Old gold words
toned like concert violins,
tuned to talk to God.

After the French and Latin wars
I relished the poppies of Donne
though I thought this graceful foreign tongue
was only meant for men—
all right for the likes of Coleridge
but it gave me unpleasant dreams.

They say we cannot speak it
and they are right.

It was hard and slippery as pebbles,
full of cornered consonants
and pinched vowels, all said
from the front of the mouth—
no softness, no sorrow,
no sweet lullabies—
until we took it by the neck and shook it.

We sheared it, carded it fleeced it
and finally wove it
into something of our own,
fit for curses and blessings
for sweet talk and spite,
and the sound of hearts rending,
the sound of hearts tearing.

X

THE VIGIL

Under a whale humped hill
on a still night with moonlight
a young girl cannot sleep.
Something in her belly stirs
and draws her out
to stare at the shiny sea,
the ghostly beach. She is waiting
for pirates with black hair.
When no-one comes
she reaches under her pillow
for a book without a heroine.

She is landbound,
lately kept from the sea
by men that know their lives hang
on such a thing as luck in a boat.

GHOST

There is little mention here
of grandmothers and mothers
for this is the book
of fishermen and Englishmen.
They hounded me and minded me,
they shone like gods for me
and burned all others out of the sky.

One man at home among visions,
one not given to ghosts;
one that wrote of bravery and drowning,
one that lived it.

What could she do to match them?
She heard only the cries
out of the night depths,
the sighs of the unclaimed drowned
haunted her bedroom at the gable end.

She was sure that some awful sight,
a soaked soul,
would break the night waters
below Doon Hill and come to her
shivering in the moonlight
to plead for burial.

After a frozen moment
she would shimmer and dissolve
like stained glass in a fire,
leaving a blot
like an unconfessable sin,
a black spot on the tongue.

xii

THE FORGE

Standing at the smithy door
in the long evenings, I learned
that the shape of things
is forged in fire. My fingers
itched for the bellows
and the first pangs
of forbidden attraction stirred,
a slight pitch in the ground.

Oh I do not want to remember
how the first nail
was driven into a hoof,
the horse's suppliant eyes, how
you only had one chance.

No, I do not want to remember
how the blushing, bending iron
soughed and turned black
as it was plunged into heavy water
by the maker's unwavering hand.

I do not want to know
that this is the way of things,
that only pain bestows
the right to speak of life
and I am no good
at bending with the wind.

I am older now. I know
they did not lie when they said
what will not bend will break.
They did not lie
or else I was too weak.

II - *The Cave*

"The tribes merged into the hills,
The ultimate rocks where seals converse."

John Montague
'The Rough Field'

CORNERED

As a child, were you dark or fair?
The innocent question gaffed her.

I was a dark child, and frail.
I never warmed to land

but if anyone menaced my shore
I would tooth and claw and nail

for the only thing I had,
an undiscovered continent

of swirly forests and scant
unwinding sheets of sand.

AT THE BLESSED WELL

Beyond the end of the road
where only hungry sheep and pilgrims
know what lies between them
and the grey Atlantic
two stone mounds mark time.

Earnest at thirteen
in her thin dress and thick coat
she shivered off her shoes.
Her feet shrivelled and turned
a faint blackberry blue
on the thirteenth of November.

Seven circles, sure, slow
as each one joined she threw
a stone into the well. The shale
gleamed with frost, and pennies
from people who had nothing
lay greening on holy ground
but the well, they said
was always warm and often cured.

She circled seven times, certain
of her saint. Little bracelets
of ripples edged the water.
Below the sea raged.
Her feet on fire she told
prescribed prayers for fortitude
deliverance and a happy death.

Rebelling at the last station
she risked it all and begged Cailín
for a little palace in the sun,
the kind that nestles between the covers
of her hundred and one nights.

The seventh stone dropped in.
It disappeared like a confessed sin.
Cleansed, she ran up the jagged hill.
It's not cold, not cold at all
she called, determined for a miracle.

The Swim

She goat-stepped over crags
to sanctuary, a stony beach
roundy for bare feet
with a necklace of squelchy seaweed.

The water was greeny clean,
delicious on her legs.
She dipped her fingers next
to bless herself against drowning,
then held her breath and dived
to the root of a shallow rock.

Delighted at the first body shock
she flipped her golden scaled tail
and floated in her grassy room
unreachable, unseen.

There have been other swims
in other oceans, naked at midnight
and warm. There is only one womb.

MOYNE PARK

i.m. George Macbeth

"Cad a dheanfaimid feasta gan adhmad?
Ta deireadh na gcoillte ar lar;"

Cill Cais

The heart is still in the great house.
You graced it with an interval of decency.
Fine-plumed to the end like the doomed swan
beating its way through a blinding storm
to crash against the quivering glass
you sat, beating out your last breath
in sonnets, silent in a golden morning room,
avoiding nothing; your marriage of manners and rage.

But the life, George! We who were dispossessed
made free in borrowed elegance, made an entrance
and silently I exulted. From those high cold rooms
any of us could have ridden forth, sleek with assurance.
When you left, the house died. I will not mourn it.
Thanks to you, I would no longer burn it.

TÍR EOGHAIN

'Now' you said, 'let's talk
about what feels good.' So we walked,
listing small furry animals, the shimmer
of money in your hands and summer water.

At nine, your high American voice
already holds another's coolness,
a taste of what it will become,
here where the moon only courts darkness.

Rafting between nightfall and the shore
I know only that this is the lake
where poets stumble and sleep.
Already you have surveyed it

and declared yourself prince
of the small islands. You appoint
me keeper of the privy purse
with a currency of bottle tops.

For all your business sense
you are child enough for my lap
when you tire. Your thin arm slips
from my shoulder in sleep.

Whenever I think of you
there is gold rippling through
your small fingers like mercury,
like fleece, like warm snow.

THE PRICE OF SILK IS PAID IN STONE

O sweet romance in Connemara!
A soft day, a speckled hill,
a mirror bay, all certain
as the mountains swollen with heather.
All transient as thrushes' eggs,
the wild water
and a streaked chameleon sky.

O no romance in Connemara.
A speckled hen
fasting under a basket,
a whetted knife and the danse macabre,
the musk of feathers in the Sunday stew.

Yes, and when you lack the guts
to wield the knife
what use is it to the hungry child
that you dwell in gossamer and dusk?
Let them find out early
that love has a bitter edge
when life is lived among the rocks.

Yet I have seen the sedge
burn with slow fire.
I have seen the lakes rise
and make swirls of silk
in the October sky.

O the price of leaving,
the cost of coming home.

The Countrywoman Remembers

The West is hard
with a treacherous yielding,
so sometimes in summer
there is softness.

The mountains stand
peaked against the sky
the colour of blue rock,
a lake scooped into a bog

reflects the breast
of an unsuspecting hill
and once, no lie,
an apricot moon hung

low in the night
like forbidden fruit.
These are the dangerous things,
the lovely, lovely faces of pain,

the soft temptations.
They used to make me wonder
until I learned the cost, before
they taught me to trust
the surer comforts of stone.

WEAKNESS

I come from a line of strong women
mostly dark, all carved from a harder rock
than me. I am the thin fault
that runs through the seam, a wave of quartz
surfing through granite, condemned to masquerade.
I am where history breaks and divides.
Brittle and weak, I have been cast down
before the upright women of my tribe,
ashamed before their silent eyes.

I carry weakness like a plague of tears.
They ignore it with the unassailable
mercy of their gaze that has not wavered once
in six thousand years and never lies—
only the strong survive. I am spared
for a doubtful task. They bear me up,
knowing I am only fit for dreams.
There I live mostly, avoiding funerals,
tracking the shapes that wheel across their heavens.

Nightly I enter the dark cave's mouth
where waves of whispering women
clamour to be heard. Surf brushes sand
in a softer language, the only tender thing
they had. The thread of my grandmother's voice
guides me through a labyrinth of syllables.
She knows my tendency to wander and get lost.
Daily I unravel voices from a choir of ghosts
and transcribe the blazing cyphers of my past.

CANTO JUNDO

On New Year's Eve I walked the strand alone
in need of salt. The wind stinging my face
knew me. The sea was green and mountainous
and mine. I faced it fearless and my own
deep song merged with a surge in the blood.
It flowed, rose and broke loud on the winter shore.

Behind me a nimbus of woods
and honeyed sunsets hazed.
Eight years of Latin words drifted,
coloured bottles on the waves of home.

PORPOISES
for Martin

Off Slyne Head at night
in a fifty-foot trawler
it is cold and black
even at midsummer.

The sky is close.
Out from the once manned rock
white electric light
arcs over the water.

A mysterious life pulses
under the boat. Something
disturbs the even breathing
of the waves. A sound like wings

and a shape, indiscernible
in darkness shaves the surface.
The fishermen hears
and leans over the bow.

The hairs on his neck rise
with the memory of old stories.
A school of invisible porpoises
is passing. 'Christ, they were lovely!'

Their perfect phosphorescent shapes
sculpted in the algae.

EXPLANATION

What can I tell you that's simple?
Each rock was a shade different
from the next. The sea set tangles
loose in me in winter.
It spread around me in September
an easy mother, used to changelings.

After all I was a curious child,
fond of secrets like any other.
Those whisperings among the stars
could take a lifetime to transcribe.

Go out and search the strand
for your own sign, the seed, say
of a heart shaped tamarind.
Watch how your unconscious palm
curls around its brown skin.
Call it yang snuggling to yin
in the lap of your hand.

STARTING SCHOOL

Motherless the first day
she stood alone in the empty schoolyard,
too early for fear of being late.
She stared and shrank
like a startled iris
as the sky exploded.

If she had given in and cried,
lain down on that grey rock
between the speckled cliff
and the humpy hill
she might have cried it out,
but the eldest must be strong.

Now, glancing through the kitchen window
or during a summer walk
a certain texture of stone
with no give in it drives her out
into the raw tundra of dreams.
At the edge of the horizon
between the hill and the speckled cliff
a dry-eyed child sits, frozen.

NA BEANNA BEOLA
The Twelve Pins, Connemara

Twelve guardians watched
over my child dreams
sometimes soft as peaked cream
sometimes gods of stone.
Always minding, always men.

THE CAVE

What shades will enter my dark cave tonight?
Who will the moon render powerless or strong?
What shapes? The fuss and tumble
of a Hollywood battle scene?
An unshriven soul, thin and white?
Sea virgins might even now be swimming in
with those grey ancestors of the Mac Conghaile,
the seals. The toss and tangle of shawled women
settling in for the long haul is certain.

Certain the dark hours falling silently
off all the precarious roofs of dreams,
frantic in the web of dream's unquiet authority.
Those shrill or whispering ghosts
the ancestral dead, enter nightly
claiming to be heard. They thresh the straits
of broad and slender vowels, choking on words.
My mouth is wracked like a poem
stretched between spark and shape.

'Caol le caol agus leathan le leathan [1'] mocks me.
I listen to the seals' sweet haunt
and trace its provenance. It shocks the ear.
Are these the trapped voices of the drowned
or is it the strange cry of dumb creatures
longing for something more, to be human?
Like ourselves. Always we are doomed.
I cannot put English on this,
the song of unattainable things, so I hum.

I have always lived by a sea cave
where a dark man waits, incurious.
His face, half-hidden, half-seen
is like the incipient moon, unmoved
and like the moon he watches the night unfold.
Useless to expect rescue but nonetheless
we expect it. Light. A flame
slowly turned up like an oil lamp,
eyes kindled by a swell of lost radiance.

In light the shawled women shrivel,
their incessant watching requires a veil.
The dark man, illumined is unmasked.
Once would be enough. One deep kiss
of light to eclipse the last pool of darkness
in Europe[2] and all sink back into shadow
rested, confirmed that tomorrow
will be glorious. The wait is ancient;
no God has risen from this cold sea yet.

Yet, on nights when the sky plunders
the last drops of light from the water
and waves, innocent with tangled seaweed
suck and mutter in the cave, remember
that not far from here a man broke faith;
in need of ballast for his boat
he took the chapel stones from a sacred island.
Later, heaving them overboard uneasily
he looked back and saw the stolen rocks float.

1. *A spelling rule in Irish*
2. *The philosopher Wittgenstein referred to Connemara as "the last pool of darkness in Europe".*

14TH JANUARY, 1991

Eve of the Gulf War

My father tapped the glass, virtuoso
fingers pulsing the evening's weather.
It's still high. Will it rain
tomorrow?

Did you not hear the gale warning?
Look at the sky over Slyne Head.
That needle will fall like a stone
by morning.

CEALTRACH

The children were never told
about those places. The unbreachable
silence of women protected us
from terrible things.
We heard the dread whisperings
and peopled the swarming spaces with ghosts.

Yet we never knew. They buried
unnamed innocents by the sea's edge
and in the unchurched graveyards
that straddled boundary walls. Those infants
half-human, half-soul were left
to make their own way on the night shore.

Forbidden funerals, where did mothers
do their crying in the two-roomed cottages
so beloved of those Irish times?
Never in front of the living children.
Where then? In the haggard, the cowshed,
the shadowed alcoves of their church?

That Christian religion was hard.
It mortified the flesh
and left mothers lying empty,
their full breasts aching, forever afraid
of what the winter storms might yield,
their own dreams turning on them like dogs.

THE STORM

A spray of red carnations on the sill.
A fire framed in limestone waxes
in my semi-detached living room.

The habitual inventory of my men,
who is running for shore
who safe on what island, completes me.

I am waiting for the storm
and all the boats are in.
For two days I have bowstringed.

A humming deep in the ocean
vibrates me like a high tuned violin.
Every muscle, drawn like wire, sizzles.

The wind rises. Locked in woodlands
I hear it tuning ash and oak
as I am hauled to where the sea

is shaping new mountains. At midnight
mad airs howl like wolves
and all the trees are bending.

Swaddled in the harbour of my bed
I am rocked on seething water
absorbed in a green dance

that devours quays and laughs
at storm walls. I am a breaker
replacing beaches with boulders.

I fling wrack on a curved canvas
of ruined shore and fish drown
in my fury. The music crescendos,

ebbs, I sleep. Deep, deep, dreamless.
At evening I survey my redrawn beaches
satisfying new sand with footsteps.

The waning moon hushes me home
where I am needed and Handel
is flowing from the radio.

WORK
After Montague

i

From Moycullen we drive
past the surviving woods.
The wind or approaching winter
has quenched the flame-tree in Oughterard.

The bog is turning umber in licks
wind buffets us and cloud
tatters to rain across the hills.
What harm. I was raised to weather this.

ii

Packages of hay heat-sealed in plastic
have saved some farmer's labour.
They give way to pitchforked stacks
capped in old bags.

They are pushing us towards Brussels,
golf courses and ugly hotels,
the feasibility of others' leisure—
they say this is good for us.

Sure enough, no sane woman
would trade a plumbed bungalow
for a consumptive cottage.
Some things have improved.

Yet there is dangerous loss,
hanging like an unpainted Angelus.
We are going to pay our last respects
to the blacksmith. He worked

with definite tools, the hammer,
the anvil and tongs. They rang like bells
and sparks flew everywhere
from the hooves of newly shod horses

striking the road. They bellowed
out of the coals and rose
from hot white iron struck
on the anvil when the forge

was a crucible, furious with the energy
of things being made—useful, a solid grate,
beautiful, a Fabergé gate. A child watched.
she did not touch. This was real work,

holy somehow. The memories blaze
and realise. I have been mourning
for three days not what is gone
but the shape of what is left.

SAVING THE TURF
for Leo Hallissey

Once we were like Synge's peasants,
harvesting wilderness with a sleán,
too tired from bearing and rearing
to count wild flowers,

tired keeping the slow fires
and watching children die or go
through the flaming furze.
We only notice what is scarce.

Now we know the bog road is where
fire and water meet, and burn.
This is no place to be alone at night
when dark shapes rise and quietly move,

our immigrant host. Briefly released
from footing real estate in Boston,
they swim through a rent in politicians' dreams,
the wild Irish, civilised and gone.

They are circling over the smouldering bog,
nightbirds, calling for something lost.

THE FIDDLE PLAYER

He cradles the fiddle to his chin
tucking it in like a child
and a hawthorn bends with blackbirds.

As he hefts the bow, tests the air
for sweetness or unremembered ghosts
silver flashes in a clean river.

The bow quivers for an instant,
light as the last sliver of day
over the Corrib; will he make us dance

or draw all our unsaid sorrows
into one lamenting call
to ebb and flow and soothe us?

He strikes the first note;
birds fly, feet tap and three trout
clear the furious waterfall.

THE QUILT

It was a plain house but for the quilt
that lay on your brass bed, waiting
like a storybook. Your fine stitches
portioned the fields like stone walls,
no two the same but the right shape
on everything in the end.

I have it still, a gallery of memories,
old rose for the first child,
the day you got married in ivory,
the long purple stretch before he died.
This is no calendar of ordinary time.

That scatter of bluebells I was seven
and primroses circle the path
that brought you to New York and back
to preside over my childhood.

You worked hard at that brown ridge
in a mossy ripple of lazybeds
and the wild orchids are when
you were seventeen. There is a splash
of yellow stars tiny as needleyes
on a navy sky and a tempting sliver
of new moon hangs among
the gathering shades of your last winter.

Always one to finish things
you bordered it in blue
the colour of delft, ageless colour
of devotion to Herself, God's mother.

DRIVEN

She left his bed one wild night
and put on her wedding dress.
They knew what happened by the trail
of snagged lace, ivory blossoms on the furze.

She escaped him in one long plunge
into a crazed sea. The women cried –
Her poor torn dress. That crowd
all had a mad streak a mile wide, he said.

There were always wives who left,
their stories only snatches in the air
but over Slyne Head the last light
is meshed in the tracks of their flight.

It is time to elevate this host
of women. A bare feathering of air
disturbs the ear. In dreams too deep
to remember they call us and we hear.

We swim down into the murk
and wake perturbed, our minds adrift
among the wreckage. One by one
they must leave again. By water, by rope, by cliff.

LIADAN WITH A MORTGAGE
BRIEFLY TASTES THE STARS

Breasting the hill, she pauses and looks down.
In the stillness, her children sleep. She sees lights
winking in Mayo, Croagh Patrick
invisible to the right, her husband inside reading.

The house, anchored at the edge of the world
is solid, comforting. Oh, she thinks,
have we really been our own architects?

The earth gurgles as last night's rain seeps
to its subterranean level.
She would hate to live on dry land.
The house pulses like amber. It is warm
and the weather, settling at last
unsettles her. Those treacherous Septembers!

There are mounds of soft fruit ripening,
waiting to be preserved. She sees
plum and damson staining the clouds. This year
there will be no harvesting. Let those colours
ache and deepen into havoc –
she is not responsible.

A cat whispers past her feet, nightstalking.
She smiles
and sheds her garments, a light blouse and skirt
then slips into the watered sky

and holds it for a moment to her skin,
all moisture
a dress to go wandering out beyond the stars in,
stravaiging among the planets
like Zeus's daughter.
She could take in the whole universe tonight.

The house is oblivious, its roots
pierce the bedrock. Although she is glad
some god made a woman of her
she will acquiesce and go in. She dresses
and walks to her back door, quieted for now.
To the east a garnet moon rises.

TRACING
for my father and Richard Murphy

They sit under a western window
a poet and a fisherman
tracing the genealogy of pucáns. Back
to the summer of nineteen-twenty-seven,
back to a rotting template in the sand.
Between them they could raise the dead.

And I forever outside looking in
am thinking of women measuring
the rising skirts of the wind, scanning
the swollen sea for one speck
to lift out of a trough,
a miracle of engine or sail

when I would rather be there
beside the black-haired men,
appeasing God with the swift sacrifice
of net to knife. What keeps me out,
the uncontented daughter?

The lines are drawn, life's soundings
etched across my face. What's underneath,
the cleansed bone, is defined below
that inner sea of age and jealousy
and rage at all the sunrises
missed in sleep. Was I betrayed by tears
or a thirst for the tender word?

I feel the heft of a satin handled
fish-knife. The poem forms,
a lobster pot turning
on a wooden wheel. The slats
are pliant and smooth. I soaked them
and peeled them bare of bark
in lessons learned under my father's eye

that things must bend to reach
a different shape. My bending
is not easy; nails are driven in.
Such work is done in winter and my hands
are pained with cold. No complaints.
He knew I wouldn't suit sewing.

Under the window I listen
to the story of a boat. They place
the keel, the boom, the tracery of ribs,
carving and caulking and laying sail.
Let me see... that would have been
nineteen-fifty-four, the year
she was born... Between them
I chart my own course and keep afloat.

III - *The Boat Poems*

"So I chose to renew her, to rebuild, to prolong
For a while the spliced yards of yesterday."

Richard Murphy
'The Last Galway Hooker'

JEALOUSY

Look at her, the black bitch.
I see nothing beautiful.
He spends his day with her,
his nights thinking about her.
I only have peace in October
when he becomes dutiful,
a full-time husband for a stretch.

CANVAS CURRACH

I am a racer. Light, made for speed.
I hardly touch the water. Fragile
but I can carry three big men
and outlast them. It's all in the balance.
I will never drown.

I have no sail to wear but my black dress
clings to my ribs, seamless.
I am a slim greyhound of the sea.
The deeper your oars dig in
the lighter I skim.
I am built to run. Race me!

THE PATEEN

for Eileen Joyce

In Spring, in a Chicago suburb
two reddish brown butterflies
caught her unawares,
stack o'barleying around the lawn.

The discreet neighbourhood
receded in the wake
of a fey young gleoteog,[1]
swishing her skirts in the rising breeze,

clipping the waves as she swung,
easy, around the lighthouse.
The cut of her jib
was as bold as brass

when she flirted with the lapwings
winking on the shore,
though she could show respect
with the best of them,

dipping her sails to Mac Dara's bones
or slipping serenely
into whatever bay
offered berth at nightfall,

all feigned indifference
under a sky streaked prettily
for tomorrow's storm.
That was the free and dancing time

before she was landlocked,
when America was a dream
and every Sunday in summer
was race day, before the tide turned.

1. *A type of traditional sailing craft.*

PUCAN
The American Mor

i

My years of work, the hard times
of drawing black bog
from Connemara to Inis Oirr and Clare
to keep the fire in winter burning
like women everywhere, are over.

I am prized as a racehorse now
with the same crowd
claiming to judge my flesh.
What would they know about the likes of me?
I that have been steered
by gentlemen and the odd brute
gave my best always
to the men that let me have my head
and matched me, and they were few.

I have watched the fire
flicker and die in young men
and seen fierce men learn content
and grow mellow as turfsmoke

as I have learned
that boys still bleed to death
in this world of fast cars and trawlers
with telephones and dry beds.

ii

Many a crew has gone
with no work to hold them.
I wonder what race they run
on the streets of Boston or New York,
what life there could be
for those born to the sea
building tunnels under it.

I remain, older and more beautiful.
I am the Queen, mistress of old men
and young men still, and men that were lost.
Dressed more lovingly than any wife,

each tuck and seam is adjusted
to my frame though the cut is ancient
and the colour, either rusty red or white
suits me. I am blessed by priests.

Quiet water still slides
along my flanks, silkily.
But when the heart of the sea
pulses its waves under me
and the wind breathes
a woman's shape into my sails
then I am loveliest.

With the right hand
to channel me between grasping rocks
like Grannuaile before me
I could leave these tangled bays
and make the coast of Portugal.

THE MAIGHDEAN MHARA

It is always the same,
the men say little and the women talk,
guessing what the men are saying
in the long gaps between words.
Always fishing for clues
they drop barbs, make humorous casts
in an endless monologue of lures.
They'll say anything for a bite.
The men look hunted and stay silent.

But I can make them sing out
a shower of curses and commands.
I challenge them to win
against the sea and other men.
They listen for the slightest whisper
between me and the wind. They understand
my lightest sigh, and respond.

Here in my belly where men feel safe
I draw out their soft talk,
rising, falling, low as breath.
At ease and sure of their control
they are, in Irish, eloquent.
I never let on anything
but fall and rise and humour them.

Out of History

To observe the enigma of marked time
      take a woman
from the sixteenth century.
      It took one unexecuted stroke
to write her out of history
      and three hundred years
of unrelenting song to write her in.

The story swells
      across a chorus of generations
and dwindles to one quiet voice,
      father to female child.

Then all that is required
      against history's scheming
is one thin excluded daughter
      sitting on a rock
with the sea pounding,
      a scant coat that may become a cloak
and a flotilla of trawlers or caravelles
      dancing on her laughter.

IV - *The Grannuaile Poems*

*"out of myth into history I move to be
part of that ordeal
whose darkness is*

*only now reaching me from these fields,
those rivers, those roads clotted as
firmaments with the dead."*

Eavan Boland
'Outside History'

I am Gráinne, Queen of men,
mistress of a thousand ships,
Bunowen's chatelaine.
A working mother,
I keep my maiden name.

GRAINNE'S PRAYER TO THE TWO VIRGINS

i

You might master me
in the territory of shared beds
but out here by the brown bog
I will watch and see
if the terror of a sea cave
seduces you, how you will be
when your Spanish city
recedes like a rip-tide.

What comfort will you reach for
in the shore night
when the moon's accusing light
exposes your secrets,
little naked molluscs
slithering in fright.

This is where I come into my own
having long known
how to harvest green light.
I mesh the phosphorescent flashes
winkle-picking silver fishes
under a net of stars.

Can you keep the compass points
of your finely tutored mind
from flying to opposite poles

of the gyrating planets?
Are you after all a man
that knows Pisces from Scorpio?

ii

If you are I am finished.
The long love poem will begin.

> *Maria, help me to avoid*
> *the merciless mapping of the end*
> *when every footstep is counted*
> *and the curve of his mouth*
> *turns cruel and burns on my skin.*

> *Since it is the way of women*
> *to talk of love, tell me again*
> *how I will know, how*
> *I will do nothing and nothing*
> *but hunger will grow.*
> *Will it be his eyes, scudding*
> *across my face or his voice*
> *hardening like arteries, the heat*
> *slowly going down and only loss,*
> *a woman's legacy in this place*
> *true to its promise?*

That you may fail me now
while there is still time.
That every vision and rock
in the haunted moonscape of the bog

may stir uneasy in your sleep
and mark you coward,
another Spanish fighting cock
for me to scorn.

That the untender winter dark
may unman you and drive you out.

But what if you stay
gentling the cold moon with your talk,
making me soft, a slave?

> *O Bríd, protect me from love*
> *the treachery stirring in my own heart.*

St Brigid's Windfall

So this is love—your step
on the watery stair,
the sheepskin nuzzling our feet,
a kept flame in a tower
and nothing to repent.

I am the ripening moon
like other women at last
glowing under your hand.
Now the hopeless war is past
I sleep content.

LOSS

Dead. Slaughtered like a stag
on a hill. Young,
water brought. There will be
no more room for men.
White. What is this
waxen work they bring me?

I will not touch that face
for a dead kiss.
I will not reach for your hands
to hold them and feel them cold.
This torn thing is not
your breast. Dead?
Where are you gone?

Am I to become the woman
that hath imprudently passed
the part of womanhood
like steel through fire?
The flame has died
and something cold is made.
I will be terrible in old age.

Your breast is torn.
The heat is gone.
Now I have no-one to mind me
and keep me warm.
Only your dark ghost
and the sea at night singing
of blood and empty orange groves.

CASTAWAY

They call me a pirate queen
a hard woman, mean
as any man. How do they know?
I was born able to read
the weather. What chance had I?
A gift they said. Yes, like a sword.

Didn't I want to sit
with other women by the fire
talking about children and robes,
the best way to play up to a husband?
Women were always too strong
for me. They flashed smiles
laced with messages in code.
I never broke it.
There was some sign I didn't know
that kept the circle closed.

And the bitches lied. I never had a man
able to mind me since I was a child.
It was mostly fools that tried.
They wouldn't let me alone
to see would I come to them.

Except one. Brief. Gone.
I snatched him from Achill Sound,
a Spanish Grandee! He rose
out of a storm like a god

to claim me. I was a queen then
and if the weather left me alone
I took pleasure in my bed.

I slept deep as the swell
off Dún Aengus that long summer.

Maybe the sea yielded her treasure
jealously. One summer was all I had.
When storms started in my blood again
what could I do but run with them
on every tide or drown.

GRAINNE'S ANSWER TO BURKE'S PROPOSAL

Take me for one year certain
hot and cold and strong.
What woman will give you
as much for that long?
A year in a wild place.
Take me or leave me as I am.

PRAYER

Let my breath rise.
From the gilded contours of the hills,
from the boiling sea,
from the rock of Slyne Head
let the light mesh with wind
and quench hell for me.

That a seventh wave
may pitch and toss and carry me
senseless through the coming storm
but if I am to drown
drink me deep.
Do not take me on the undertow
but rising the steep
green plane of inhalation,
poised to whisper a name,
a plea, a floating incantation.